This book belongs to:

_____

Author: A.R. Turner

Co-author: Amy Butler

Co-author: Brant Turner

Copyright © 2024

All rights reserved.

ISBN: 979-8-9902301-0-1

Printed in United States

First Edition: February 2024

About the Authors

Meet A.R. Turner, Amy R. Butler, and Brant W. Turner—the creative minds behind this delightful children's book. With their combined experience of over 50 years in elementary education and medical science, they have dedicated their lives to shaping young minds.

Why This Book Matters

Imagine a lifeline—a bridge that connects eager learners to the essential building blocks of the English language. That is precisely what this book aims to be. It is like a compass guiding children through the vast ocean of language learning.

The Journey Ahead

As you dive into these pages, you will discover a kinesthetic and tactile approach to learning. We believe that association, movement, and touch are powerful tools. They will help young learners swiftly master the first steps of reading and writing in English.

So, let's embark on this exciting adventure together!

Introduction

Begin a wonderful learning journey with this alphabet coloring and handwriting practice workbook. This comprehensive workbook will engage the child in learning the alphabet with enthusiasm and a smile on their face. An effective way to teach the alphabet is to start with capital letters, then teach lowercase letters. When using this system, the child will quickly learn to recognize the letters and sounds as they color twenty-six large and unique images.

This workbook enhances the young learner's tactile and kinesthetic learning experiences. Teachers and parents can make the letters come alive for the child with the teaching tips, movements, and stories for each letter. Adding movements, associations, and sounds with practice is a more effective way to learn than repetition and memorization. Children can also practice writing and improving their motor skills by tracing the letters.

This teaching and letter recognition system is highly effective for all learners including challenged learners, exceptional learners, and English language learners.

The authors of this workbook include two experienced elementary education teachers and a medical professional with a Master of Medical Science.

Workbook Features

Parents, teachers, and young learners will enjoy working together while engaging in the following features of this book:

- Large Illustrations: Each capital letter is embedded in a cheerful and engaging image to aid the learner in letter recognition and sound association. Letter recognition is reinforced by allowing the learner to color the image.
- Teaching tips for each letter: Practical ways to use tactile and kinesthetic reinforcements are given through the movement instructions for each letter.
- Engaging stories: Each letter has a unique short story that contains letter repetition. This will help children associate the letters and their sounds with words in the story.
- Tracing letter templates: Multiple practice pages are available for letter tracing.
- Blank practice lines: Empty lines are available to practice writing letters.
- Graphic layout design: The "8.5 x 11" layout and design of this book allows for large images. The tracing lines allow the learner ample space for practice.

Letter A

When introducing the capital letter A, point to the letter and tell the child this is the capital letter A. Repeat the name of the letter and then pronounce the sound of the letter A. Next, have the child trace the capital letter A on the page with their finger. Then have them practice saying the sound of the letter A several times.

Movement

Discuss with the child that arrows can be used in everyday life. (clocks, tools, directions) Find examples if possible. Ask them to close their hands together and practice pointing them away from their body in the shape of an arrow. Read and discuss the story about Ace Arrow. Then ask them to color the picture.

Story

Ace is always looking for arrows. On his way to school he sees road signs with arrows. At school he sees arrows in the parking lot and arrows in the hall. At home, Ace sees arrows moving on his clock. In his back yard, Ace shoots his bow and arrow at the acorn tree. There are arrows all around us. Help Ace look for more arrows.

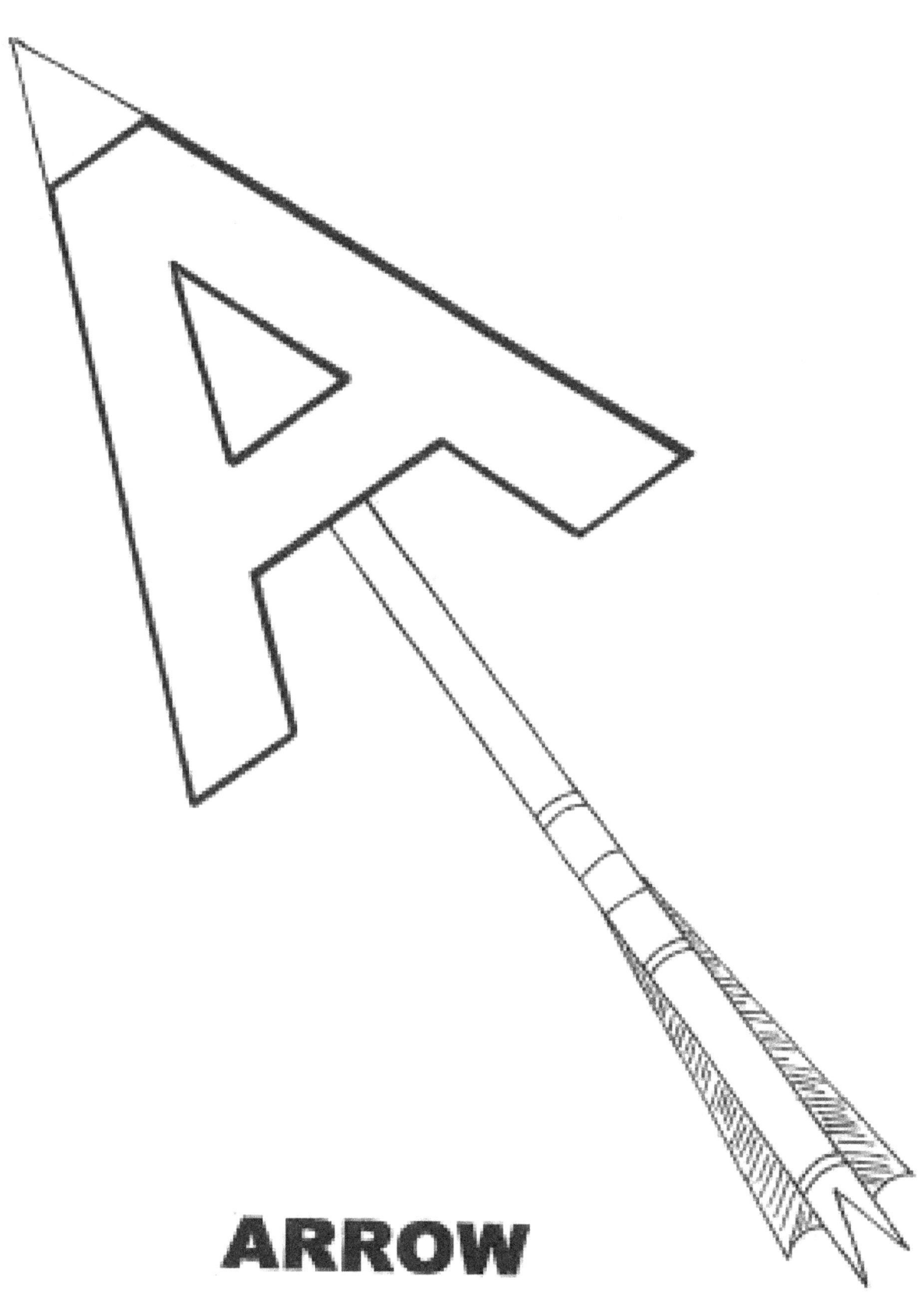

ARROW

Letter B

When introducing the capital letter B, point to the letter and tell the child this is the capital letter B. Repeat the name of the letter and then pronounce the sound of the letter B. Next, have the chilld trace the capital letter B on the page with their finger. Then have them practice saying the sound for the letter B several times.

Movement

Explain to the child that a bee buzzes and bounces from flower to flower to get food. Their buzzing sound shakes yellow pollen off the flower for the bee to eat. Ask the child to make a buzzing sound while pretending to fly like a bee getting its food. Read and discuss the story about Bouncy Bee. Then have them color the picture.

Story

Bouncy Bee buzzes all day long for her food. Bouncy Bee's favorite flowers are yellow buttercups. Bouncy Bee collects all the food she needs from the buttercups. Then she flutters her wings and buzzes back to her busy beehive.

BEE

Letter C

When introducing the letter C, point to the letter and tell the child this is the capital letter C. Repeat the name of the letter and then pronounce the sound of the letter C. Next, have the child trace the capital letter C on the page with their finger. Then ask them to practice saying the sound of the letter C several times.

Movement

Display pictures of curly hair when possible. Explain to the child that some people have straight hair, and some have curly hair. Have the child use their two index fingers to make curls in the air. Read and discuss the story about Cindy Curl. Have them color the picture.

Story

Cindy Curl cares about her curly curls. She is confident that her curls are cute. Cindy carefully brushes her curls every day. She goes to The Hair Shop when she needs her long curls trimmed. Cindy Curl looks classy with her cute curls.

CURL

Letter D

When introducing the letter D, point to the letter and tell the child this is the capital letter D. Repeat the name of the letter and then pronounce the sound of the letter D. Next, have the child trace the capital letter D on the page with their finger. Then have them practice saying the sound of the letter D several times.

Movement

Explain to the child that ducks have big feet like paddles to help them swim. Explain to them that on land, their paddle feet cause them to waddle when they walk. Have the child pretend to waddle like a duck. Read and discuss the story about Doodle Duck then color the picture.

Story

Doodle Duck loves to doodle and waddle after he is done dipping in the pond. Doodle is known in the village for his dazzling doodling. He doodles while he waddles and decorates everything he sees. Doodle Duck draws delightful attention everywhere he doodles and waddles.

DUCK

Letter E

When introducing the capital letter E, point to the letter and tell the child this is the capital letter E. Repeat the name of the letter and then pronounce the sound of the letter E. Next, have the child trace the capital letter E on the page with their finger. Then ask them to practice saying the sound of the letter E several times.

Movement

Discuss with the child foods that start with E: eggs, eggplant, edamame, and eclairs. Show them a picture of an eclair and explain that it is a pastry filled with cream. Tell them eclairs are Ethan Eats favorite dessert. If possible, find one for display. Then ask them to pretend they are eating an eclair. Read and discuss the story about Ethan Eats. Then have them color the picture.

Story

Ethan Eats wants to eat everything edible he sees. Everyday Ethan's appetite is enormous. One day he was so hungry he ate eleven eclairs all at one time. Ethan got sick and had to go the village emergency room. Now Ethan eats less desserts and more foods that are healthy for him to eat.

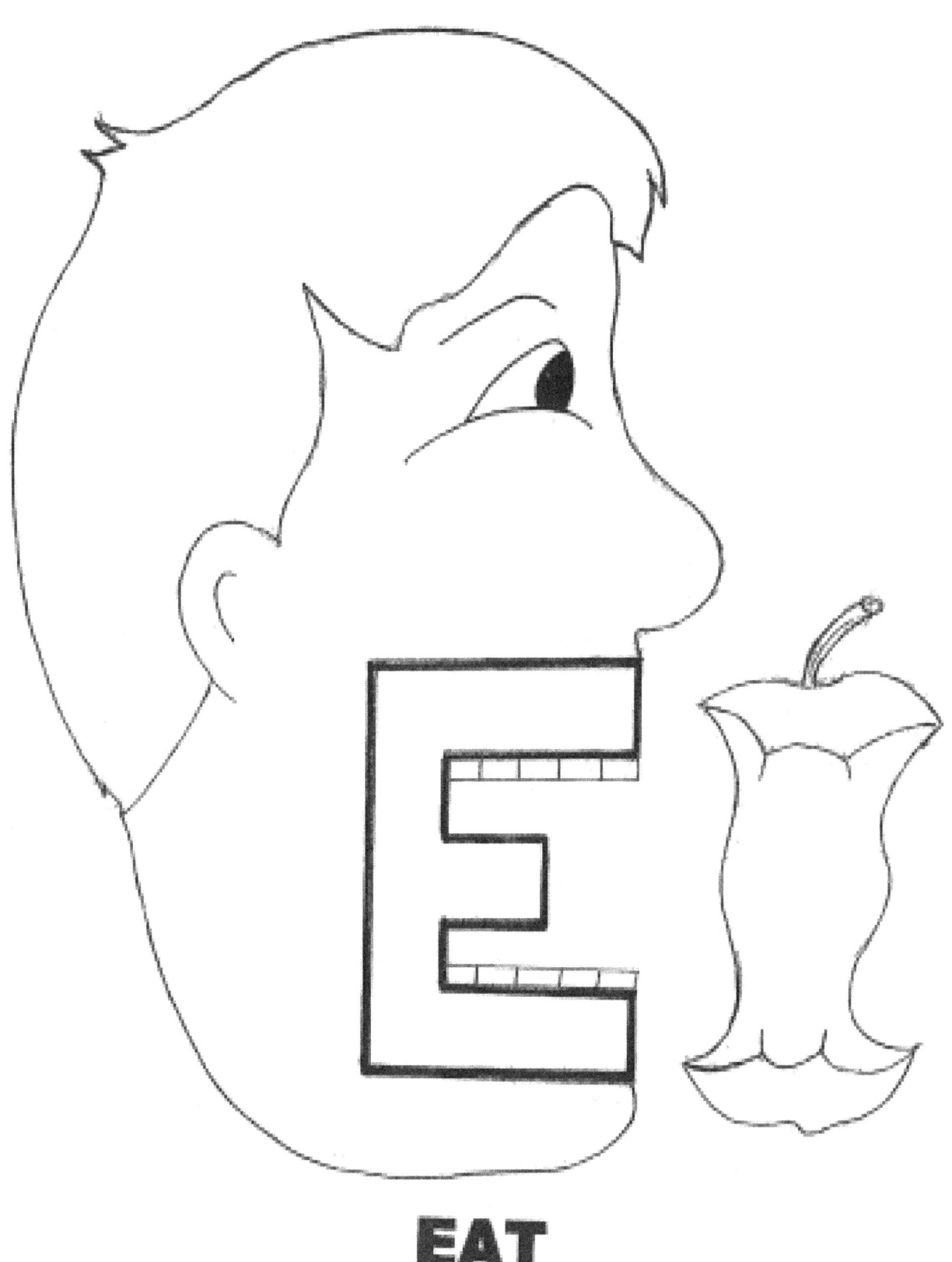

EAT

Letter F

When introducing the letter F, point to the letter and tell the child this is the capital letter F. Repeat the name of the letter and then pronounce the sound of the letter F. Next, have the child trace the letter F on the page with their finger. Then ask them to practice saying the sound for the letter F several times.

Movement

Explain to the child that a flag can flap, flow, and fly when the wind is blowing. Ask the child where they have seen a flag. Show them a real flag if possible. Then tell them they are going to hear a story about Freddy and the Flag. Read and discuss the story. Then have them color the picture.

Story

Freddy saw a large flag near the entrance to his school. The flag was flapping and fluttering in the wind. It looked like it was going to fly away. When school ended, Freddy heard the flapping sound again. It was the flag waving to Freddy as if to say, "I'll see you tomorrow." Freddy smiled and waved back at the flag.

FLAG

Letter G

When introducing the letter G, point to the letter and tell the child this is the capital letter G. Repeat the name of the letter and then pronounce the letter G. Next, have the child trace the capital letter G on the page with their finger. Then have them practice saying the sound of the letter G several times.

Movement

Have the child make a mad face like a grouch. Ask them why they think Georgie Grouch is grumpy and what they could do to make him glad. Read and discuss the story of Georgie Grouch. Then ask them to color the picture.

Story

Georgie Grouch grumbled and griped all day long. Everyday he greeted the villagers with a grouchy face. The people in the village decided it was time to help Georgie Grouch become glad. They decided to give him gifts like games, gummy bears, glue sticks, and even a pet goldfish. Georgie Grouch was incredibly glad because of all his gifts. Georgie was so grateful he changed his grouchy face to a big grin.

GROUCH

Letter H

When introducing the letter H, point to the letter and tell the child this is the capital letter H. Repeat the name of the letter and then pronounce the sound for the letter H. Next, have the child trace the letter H with their finger. Then ask them to practice saying the sound of the letter H several times.

Movement

Have the child make two L shapes with their thumbs and index fingers. Then ask them to bring their thumbs together in a way that resembles an H. Their wrists and fingers will look like a letter H. Then ask the child to think of one or more things they would find in a house that starts with the letter H. Find pictures of things found in a house that start with the letter H sound (hairbrush, hat, heater, hammock, hose, hall). Read and discuss the story about Hattie's House. Have them color the picture.

Story

Hattie and her dog Harley live in a house on Honey Lane in the village. Hattie wears her hat and hoodie to keep warm when she and Harley go to the park. When Hattie gets home, she hangs her hoodie on a hanger in the hall closet. She puts her hat on a hook in the hallway. Hattie and Harley are happy in their warm little house on Honey Lane.

HOUSE

Letter I

When introducing the letter I, point to the letter and tell the child this is the capital letter I. Repeat the name of the letter and then pronounce the sound for the letter I. Next, have the child trace the capital letter I on the page with their finger. Then have them practice saying sound of the letter I several times.

Movement

Read to the child about how icicles are formed or show them a related video. Ask them to make a snowball shape with their hand. Have them pretend their snowball is melting and icicles are forming as it melts. Ask the child to slowly open their hand and extend their fingers downward pretending they are icicles forming from the melting snowball. Read and discuss the story of Iris and the icicles. Then ask the child to color the picture.

Story

Iris lives on Ivy Lane in the village. In the cold snowy winters, lots of icicles hang from Iris's roof. One day Iris had an idea to bake a cake and put her favorite icing on top. When the cake was done, Iris sat by her window to eat her warm, delicious cake. Suddenly, Iris looked up and saw beautiful sparkling icicles melting on her roof at Ivy Lane.

ICICLE

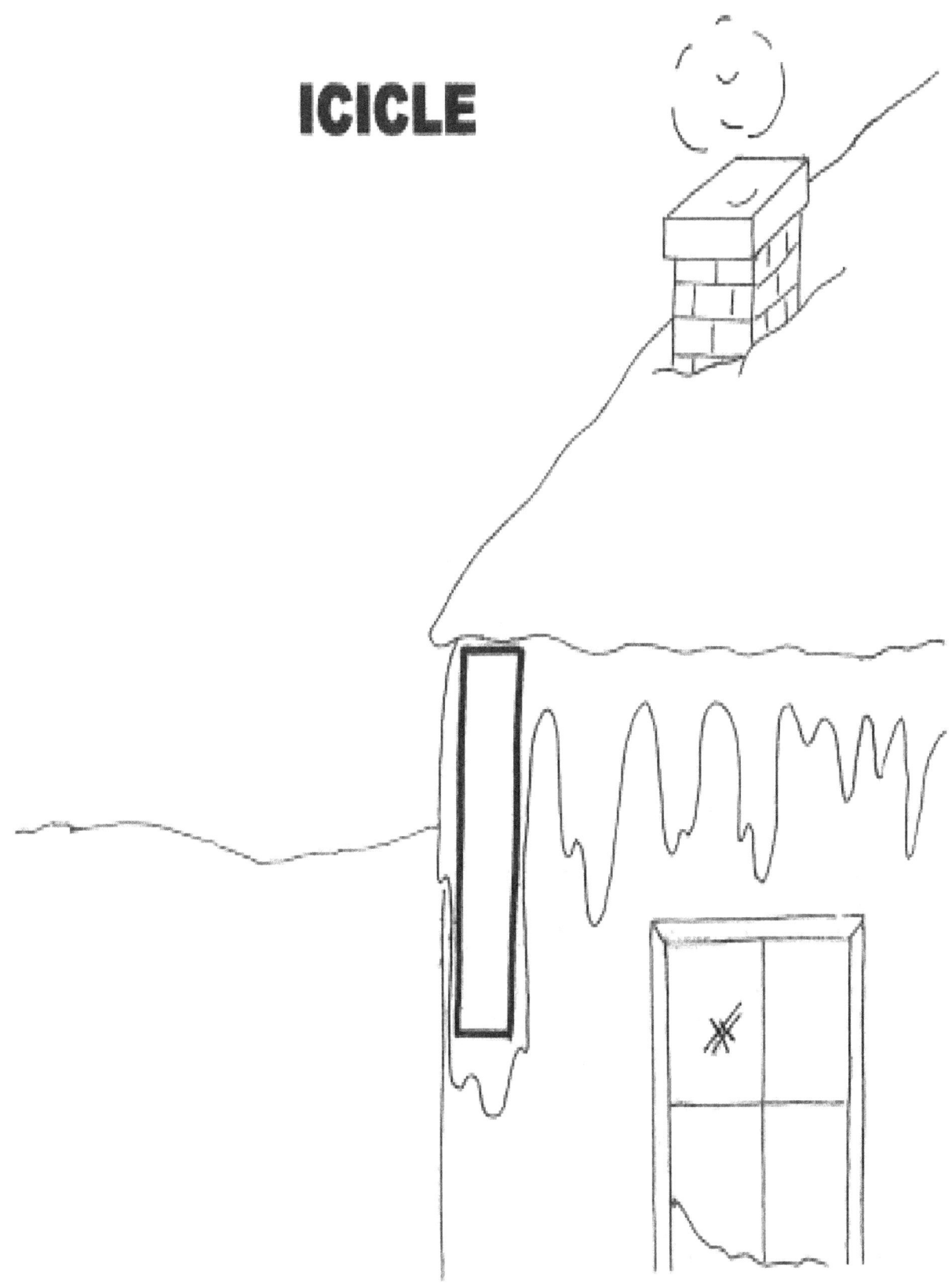

Letter J

When introducing the letter J, point to the letter and tell the child this is the capital letter J. Repeat the name of the letter and then pronounce the sound of the letter J. Next, have the child trace the capital letter J on the page with their finger. Then have them practice saying the sound of the letter J several times.

Movement

Ask the child to name living things that jump besides people and why do they jump. (frogs, most land animals, and some insects such as grasshoppers) Have the child jump in place several times while saying J is for jump. Then read and discuss the story about Jolly Jump. Ask them to color the picture.

Story

Everyone on the basketball team loves Jolly Jump. He jolts, jumps, and jams with the basketball to help his team win their games. Jolly always has a joyful smile for everyone. When Jolly is not playing basketball, he likes to jabber and joke with his friends.

JUMP

Letter K

When introducing the letter K, point to the letter and tell the child this is the capital letter K. Repeat the name of the letter and then pronounce the sound of the letter K. Next have the child trace the letter K with their finger. Then ask them to practice saying the sound of the letter K several times.

Movement

Tell the child that kicking is an important skill. Kicking is used in exercise and to reach goals in sports and other outdoor activities. Have the child pretend to kick a football or soccer ball. Next, read and discuss the story of Kenny. Then ask them to color the picture.

Story

Kenny kicks the football on the football field. Kenny kicks his best in sports. Kenny is exceedingly kind. If someone kicks or knocks Kenny over on the field, he never kicks them back. During the football games, all the people in the village cheer for Kenny because of his skills and his kindness.

KICK

Letter L

When introducing the letter L, point to the letter and tell the child this is the capital letter L. Repeat the name of the letter and then pronounce the sound of the letter L. Next, have the child trace the capital letter L on the page with their finger. Then ask them to practice saying the sound of the letter L several times.

Movement

Have the child look at their own legs and see that they are in the shape of an L. Ask them to describe what their legs can do that starts with the letter L (lift, lean). Have them go through the motion of one of these movements. Read and discuss the story about Lenny Legs. Then have the child color the picture.

Story

Lenny Legs can run faster than anyone in the village. Lenny Legs loves to run laps around Lavender Lake to prepare for the race. When he runs, Lenny is always in the lead. Lenny likes to win every race.

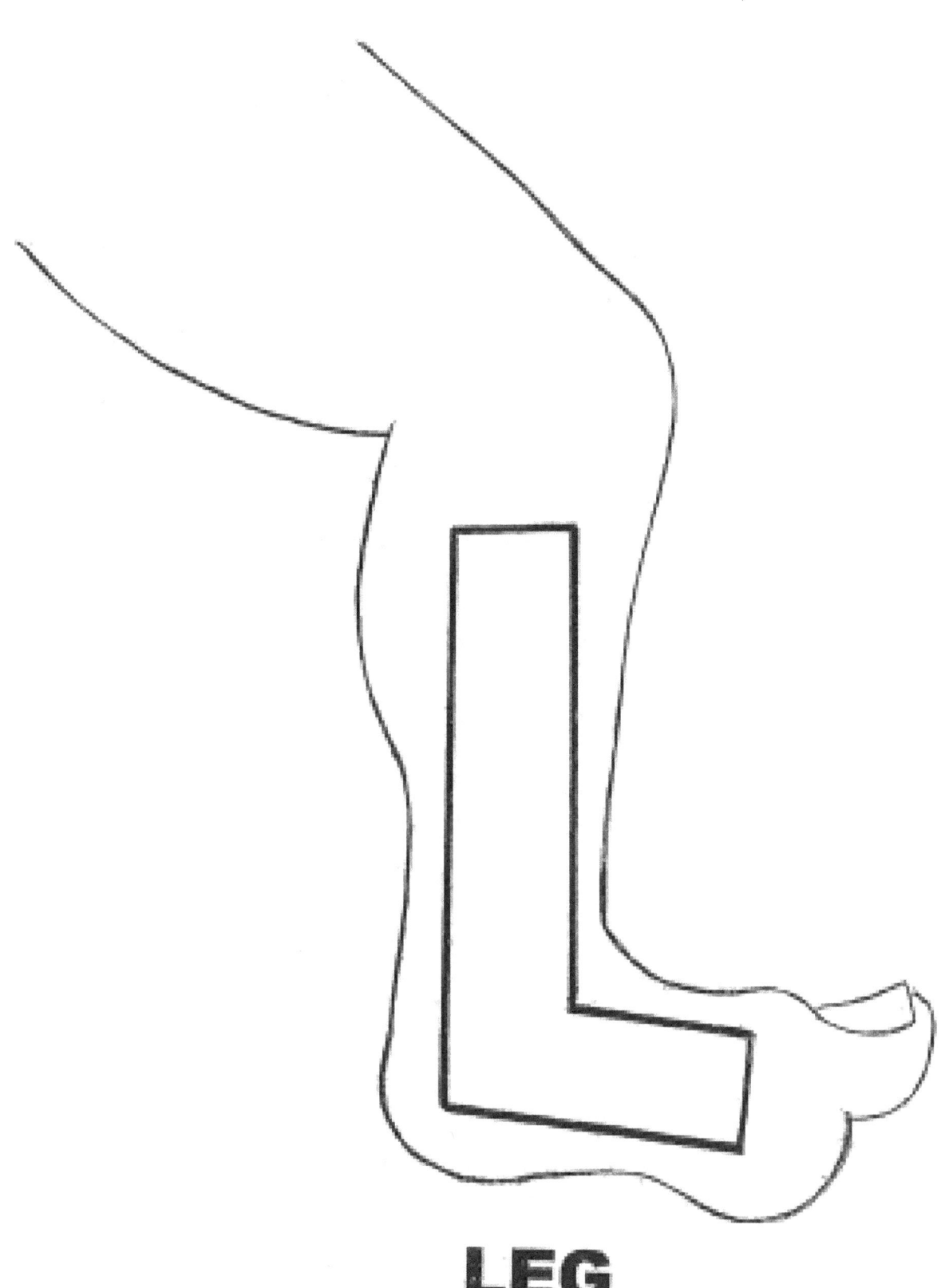

LEG

Letter M

When introducing the letter M, point to the letter and tell the child this is the capital letter M. Repeat the name of the letter and then pronounce the sound of the letter M. Next, have the child trace the capital letter M on the page with their finger. Then ask them to practice saying the sound of the letter M several times.

Movement

If the child is not familiar with mountains, show them internet pictures. Ask the child to pretend to be hiking up a steep mountain. Let them make mountains out of playdough, pencils, or some other straight objects to make the lines. Read and discuss the story about the Moss Family. Then have the child color the picture.

Story

The Moss family decided to go camping in the mountains in the month of May. They made sure to bring money and a map. Mr. Moss made a magnificent campfire. Mrs. Moss fixed delicious macaroni, and everyone roasted marshmallows. The Moss family stared at the stars until they all fell asleep in the moonlight.

MOUNTAINS

Letter N

When introducing the letter N, point to the letter and tell the child this is the capital letter N. Repeat the name of the letter and then pronounce the sound of the letter N. Next, have the child trace the capital letter N on the page with their finger. Then ask them to practice saying the sound of the letter N several times.

Movement

Tell the child that everyone has a nose. Ask them to point to their nose while saying the N sound again. Ask them to pretend to smell something with their nose. Next, read and discuss the story about Nobel Nose. Then have them color the picture.

Story

Noble Nose is the best neighbor in his neighborhood. Noble is naturally nice to everyone. He has lots of friends because he is so nice. Noble Nose is not nosey. He is a very kind and thoughtful neighbor. Noble notices when the villagers need his help. Everyone likes Noble Nose.

NOSE

Letter O

When introducing the letter O, point to the letter and tell the child this is the capital letter O. Repeat the name of the letter and then pronounce the sound of the letter O. Next, have the child trace the capital letter O on the page with their finger. Then have them practice saying the sound of the letter O several times.

Movement

Display a real orange or show an internet picture of an orange. Discuss how the shape of an orange is round like the letter O. Tell them to open their mouth in the shape of an O and say orange. Have them form the letter O by joining their thumbs and index fingers into a circle. Read and discuss the story of Odis Orange. Then have them color the picture.

Story

Odis ate only oranges for every meal. Odis's mother told him he would turn into an orange if he didn't stop eating so many oranges. One morning Odis looked into the mirror and his face was bright orange. Now Odis eats lots of other healthy foods. Odis is glad his face is no longer orange.

ORANGE

Letter P

When introducing the letter P, point to the letter and tell the child this is the capital letter P. Repeat the name of the letter and then pronounce the sound of the letter P. Next, have the child trace the capital letter P on the page with their finger. Then ask them to practice saying the sound of the letter P several times.

Movement

Ask the child to describe why pots and pans are so useful. Ask them what can be put into a pot or pan to cook. Have them pretend to be cooking and preparing vegetables that start with P in their pot/pan. (Potatoes, peas, pickles, pancakes) Read and discuss the story of Penny. Have them color the picture.

Story

Penny loves to make soup in her pot. First, she cooks the bell peppers and potatoes in a pan. Then, she adds the peas, pasta, and salt and pepper. Finally, she adds the vegetables and broth together in the pot. "Yum," says Penny, "this soup is perfectly delicious."

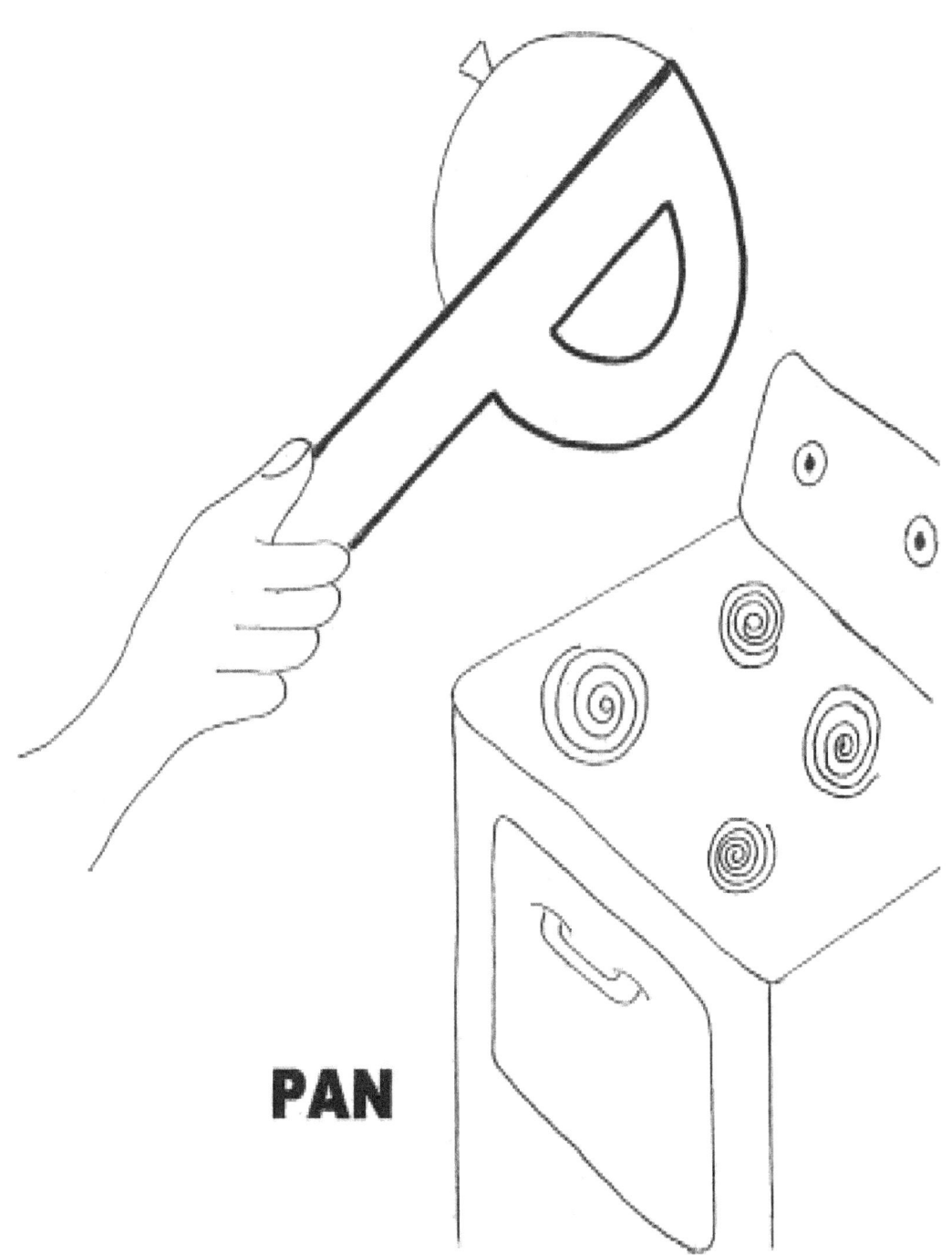

PAN

Letter Q

When introducing the letter Q, point to the letter and tell the child this is the capital letter Q. Repeat the name of the letter and then pronounce the sound of the Q. Next, have the child trace the capital letter Q on the page with their finger. Then ask them to practice saying the sound of the letter Q several times.

Movement

Explain to the child that queens are expected to look and act a certain way because they are royalty. Find internet pictures of a queen. Ask the child how they think royalty should walk and talk. Ask the child what questions they might ask a queen. Next, read and discuss the story of Queen Quilda.

Story

Queen Quilda is a good queen, but she likes to question the people in the village. She never quarrels with anyone. Sometimes she is a little silly and quirky. She wants everyone in her village to think of her as a quality queen, even though she is quirky and questions too much.

QUEEN

Letter R

When introducing the letter R, point to the letter and tell the child this is the capital letter R. Repeat the name of the letter and then pronounce the sound of the letter R. Next, ask the child to trace the capital letter R on the page with their finger. Then have them practice saying the sound of the letter R several times.

Movement

Explain to the child that running is fun to do. Tell them that you do not have to run far to run. Tell them they can quietly run in place. Demonstrate to them running in place. Next, have the child run in place. Then read and discuss the story about Randy Run. Then have them color the picture.

Story

Randy runs more than anyone in the village. He doesn't like to ride anywhere. Randy runs everywhere he goes. When it rains, Randy wears his raincoat and runs in the rain. When the villagers see Randy running, they wave and say hello. Randy waves back and keeps on running.

RUN

Letter S

When introducing the letter S, point to the letter and tell the child this is the capital letter S. Repeat the name of the letter and then pronounce the sound of the letter. Next, ask the child to trace the capital letter S on the page with their finger. Then ask them to practice saying the sound of the letter S several times.

Movement

Discuss with the child how a snake moves. Have them move slowly around the room, pretending to be a quiet, sneaky snake slithering through the woods. Have them pretend to hiss and move like a snake. Then read and discuss the story of Slyde Snake. Then color the picture.

Story

Slyde the snake is a very sneaky snake. He slithers, slides and hides in the silky grass. Slyde sees a smooth, shiny stone and slithers under it. Now he can hide and not be seen. Slyde plans his every move. He is a sneaky snake.

SNAKE

Letter T

When introducing the letter T, point to the letter and tell the child this is the capital letter T. Repeat the name of the letter and then pronounce the sound of the letter T. Next, ask the child to trace the capital letter T on the page with their finger. Then have them practice saying the sound of the letter T several times.

Movement

Have the child make a T with their two hands (finger tips of one hand touching the palm of the other flat hand) and have them repeat T is for table. Ask them to name things that start with T that could be put on a table. Examples: tacos, treats, toast, tablespoons, tangerines, teaspoons. Read and discuss the story about Tangy's Table. Have them color the picture.

Story

Tangy makes tacos for dinner on Tuesday. She eats them at her kitchen table. She uses a tablespoon to put chopped lettuce and tomatoes on her tacos. For dessert, Tangy eats taffy she bought at the village candy store. Tangy is clean and tidy. She cleans the table after

TABLE

Letter U

When introducing the letter U, point to the letter and tell the child this is the capital letter U. Repeat the name of the letter and then pronounce the sound of the letter U. Next, ask the child to trace the capital letter U with their finger. Then have them practice saying the sound of the letter U several times.

Movement

Show an internet picture of a ukulele or a video of someone playing a ukulele if possible. Have the child pretend they are holding a ukelele and ask them to strum while pretending to play. Ask them if they know any other words that start with a U. Examples: (unicycle, uniform, use) Read the story about Ugo's Ukulele. Have them color the picture.

Story

Ugo likes playing his ukulele in the village band. He is so proud of his band uniform. In his free time, Ugo rides his unicycle, a bike with one wheel. Sometimes he stops and plays his ukulele for his friends. They like to sing along with Ugo in unison. Ugo has many unique talents

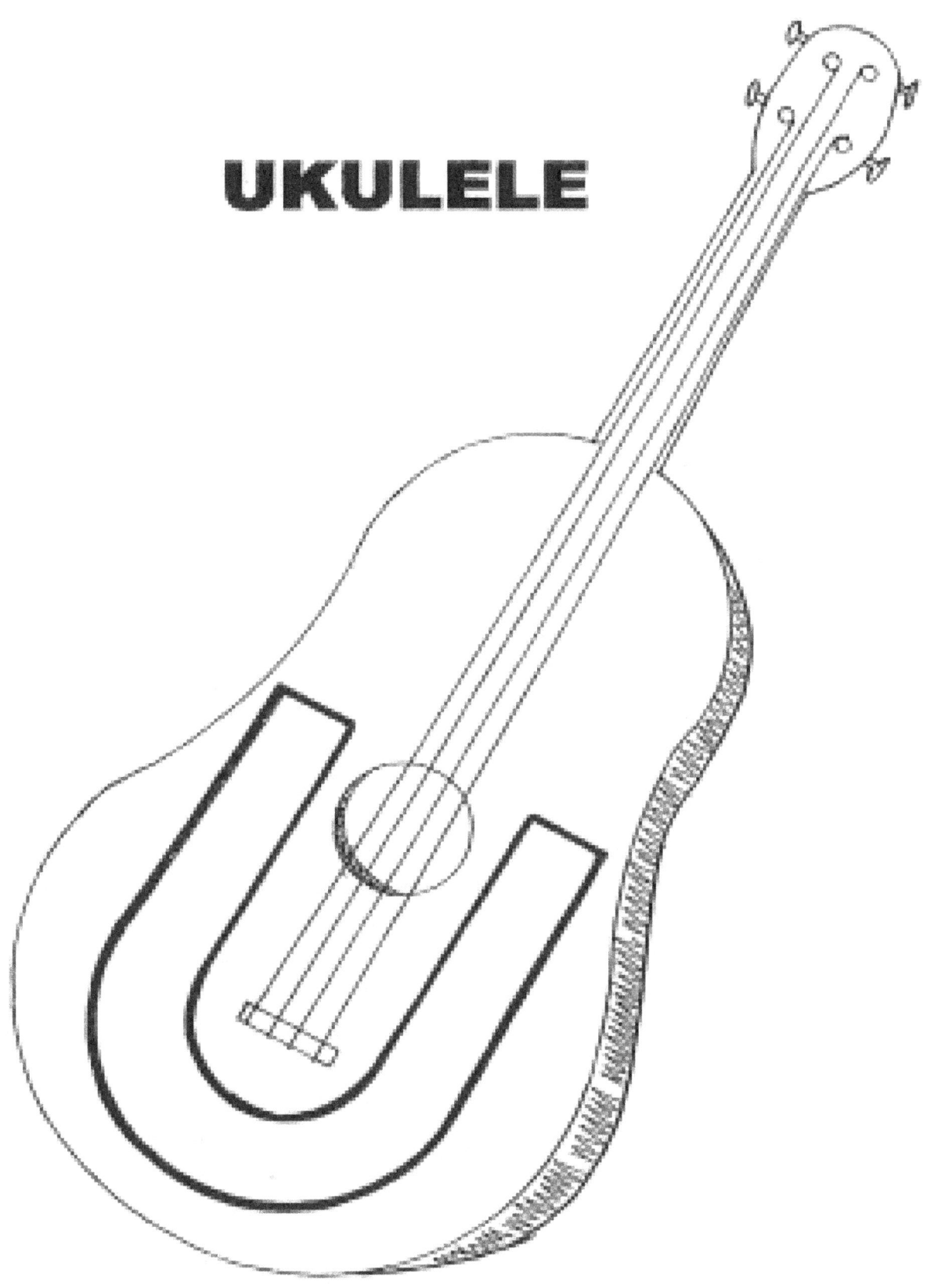

Letter V

When introducing the letter V, point to the letter and tell the child this is the capital letter V. Repeat the name of the letter and pronounce the sound of the letter V. Next, have the child trace the capital letter V on the page with their finger. Then ask them to practice the sound of the V several times.

Movement

Explain to the child what a vest is and how it is used. Show them internet pictures of different vests. Tell them anyone can wear a vest. Police officers and security guards wear a vest. Ask them to pretend putting a vest on and off while saying V is for vest. Ask the child to name other words that start with V. Examples: vacuum, valley, village, vases, villa, violets, valuables. Read and discuss the story of Venny Vest and have them color the picture.

Story

Venny owns a general store in the village. He wears a different vest every day to work. Venny sells vases, vegetables, violets, violins, and vests. Venny sells many valuable things for the villagers to buy. The villagers love Venny's General Store and the many vests he

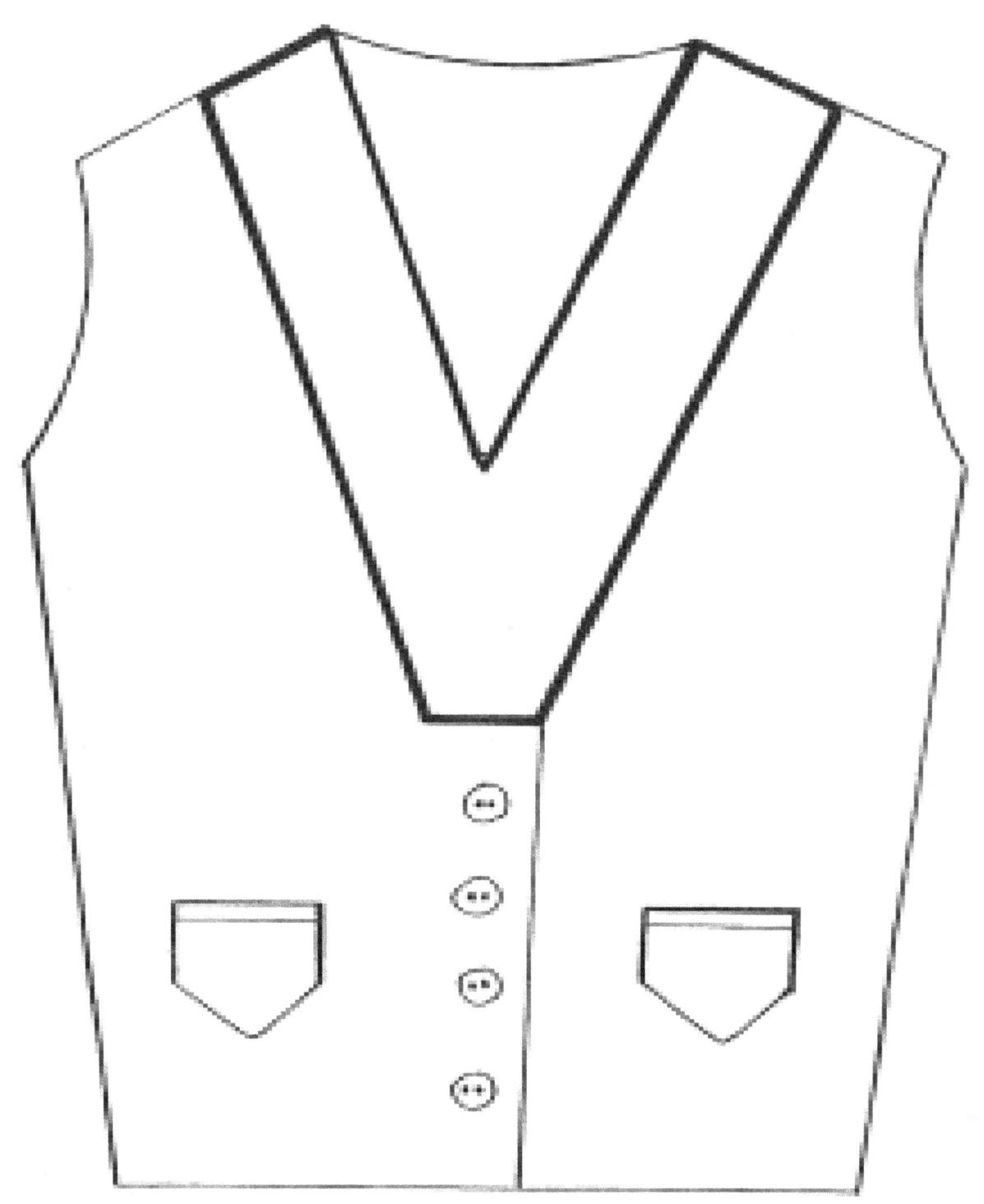
VEST

Letter W

When introducing the letter W, point to the letter and tell them this is the capital letter W. Repeat the name and the sound of the capital letter W. Next, have the child trace the capital letter W on the page with their finger. Then ask them to practice saying the sound of the letter W several times.

Movement

Ask them what birds must have to help them fly. (wings) Have them slowly wave their arms like a bird and pretend to make a flapping wing motion. Read and discuss the story of Witty Wings. Then have them color the picture.

Story

Witty is a wise old owl with big, wide wings. Witty sits on a wooden wall listening for the wind to whisper his name. Witty loves to fly with the wind to the village and visit the wishing well. At the well, Witty listens to all the villagers wonderful wishes.

WINGS

Letter X

When introducing the letter X, point to the letter and tell the child this is the capital letter X. Then repeat the name and the sound of the capital letter X. Next, have the child trace the capital letter X with their finger. Then ask them to practice saying the sound of the letter X several times.

Movement

Ask the child to cross their hands and form an X. Tell them many people cross their hands when they play the piano or the xylophone. Have them pretend to play a xylophone with their arms crossed. Read them the story about Xandy and his xylophone. Then have them color the picture.

Story

Xandy likes to play his xylophone several ways. Sometimes Xandy plays his xylophone with his hands crossed like an X. Xandy can play his xylophone with his legs crossed like an X too. Xandy plays his xylophone in the village band. He loves the letter X and even named his dog Xango.

XYLOPHONE

Letter Y

When introducing the letter Y, point to the letter and tell the child this is the capital letter Y. Repeat the name of the letter and then pronounce the sound of the capital letter Y. Next, have the child trace the capital letter Y on the page with their finger. Then ask them to practice saying the sound of the letter Y several times.

Movement

Explain to the child that a yak is a large animal that looks like a buffalo. Show internet pictures of a yak. Yaks are found in many countries. Yaks have big horns. Ask the child to hold their fingers up to resemble horns on their head. Next, have them pretend to move and grunt like a yak while holding up pretend horns. Read and discuss the story of Yippity Yak. Have them to color the picture.

Story

Yippity Yak likes to yodel, yip and yap. Yippity Yak yips and yodels all day long with the other yaks on the farm. At night Yippity starts to yawn as he walks to his yellow straw bed in the barnyard. Before he goes to sleep, Yippity Yak yawns again.

YAK

Letter Z

When introducing the letter Z, point to the letter and tell the child this is the capital letter Z. Repeat the name of the letter and then pronounce the sound of the letter Z. Next, ask the child to trace the capital letter Z on the page with their finger. Then have them practice saying the sound of the letter Z several times.

Movement

Explain to the child that a zigzag line looks like a Z. It can be used in sewing clothes together or in activities like running. Tell them sometimes roads and trails can appear to go in a zigzag direction. Ask the child to pretend to walk down a zigzag road or in the pattern of the letter Z. Read and discuss the story of Zelda. Then have them color the picture.

Story

Zelda loves to zip down the zigzag road. Today is a sunny day with zero rain. She is going to zip down the zig zag road to the zoo. On her way to the zoo, she waves to Farmer Zennie who is picking zucchini from his garden. At the zoo she visits her favorite animal, the zebra.

ZIGZAG

Additional Teaching & Practice

Rice Trace: Take a cookie sheet and pour out a bag of white rice. Spread it out evenly, then have the child write the letter in the rice with their pointer finger. You can also use this idea with colored sand instead of rice.

Letter Hunt/Letter Day: Choose one letter each day and see how many objects you can find around the home/classroom that start with the letter. Help the child recognize the object and the letter sound. Example: This is a **B**ed. What letter sound do you hear in the word **b**ed? (Make the B sound several times) If the child does not know, remind them of the bee and how it buzzes.

Bean Letters: Using dried beans, have the children form the beans into the shape of the letters. For younger children, you can write large letters on white paper and have them place or glue the beans on the lines.

Playdough Letters: Help the child to form letters out of playdough.

<u>Advanced activities</u>:

Read the room: Studies have proven that a text-rich environment for preschoolers lays the groundwork for reading success. Write the words on flash cards that begin with the letter you are focusing on. Since the book focuses on capital letters, use the capital letters for each word. Example: Book, Bed, Bottle, Bread, Butter. After writing the words on the notecards, tape them to the object. Walk them around the room and say the word to them. Then go back and let the child try to read the letter or word to you. Although the child may not understand phonic blends and word patterns, seeing the letters and the words on the object will further help them to remember the sound and recall the letters. Exposing the child to the word and its sound will help them remember the sound and word later when they are learning to read.

Recognition Games on the Go: Help your child see how text is already a part of their daily life. Show them the names of their favorite foods on the packages. Point out the letters they are learning for the day/week. Show how letters and words appear on things such as clothing labels, greeting cards, mail etc.

Play letter recognition games with your child. Ask them to name the letters in a store sign. Point to letters on packaged food items and ask them to tell you the letters. Developing text awareness should never be a chore. The more fun it can be, the quicker they learn.

Children Authors: Three- and four-year-olds can be very chatty. Take advantage of your child's interest in talking by authoring a book together. Start out with something simple, like describing a fun outing or time with friends. Staple a few pieces of paper together and write out one or two of your child's sentences on each page. If you are focusing on a letter for the day or week, use a distinct color for that letter to make it stand out in the words. Do not worry if you have yet to introduce lower case letters. This exercise is a terrific way to help the child see connections between the capital and lower-case letters. They will also be expose to hard and soft consonant sounds. Lastly, read the story back to the child and let them illustrate it.

Letter Practice & Recognition

Name the picture. Color the picture. Fill in the circle next to the letter you hear at the beginning of each word

Name the picture. Color the picture. Fill in the circle next to the letter you hear at the beginning of each word

Name the picture. Color the picture. Fill in the circle next to the letter you hear at the beginning of each word

Name the picture. Color the picture. Fill in the circle next to the letter you hear at the beginning of each word

Name the picture. Color the picture. Fill in the circle next to the letter you hear
at the beginning of each word

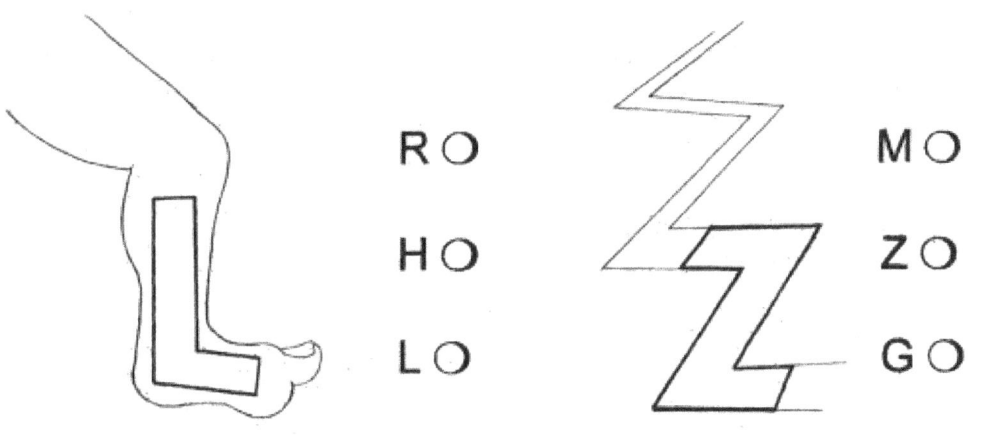

R ○   M ○

H ○   Z ○

L ○   G ○

Circle the letters in your name.

A B C D E F G

H I J K L M N

O P Q R S T U

V W X Y Z

Letter Practice & Tracing

Arrow

A A A A A A

A A A A A

A A A A A

A A A A A

Bee

B B B B B

B B B B B

B B B B B

B B B B B

Curl

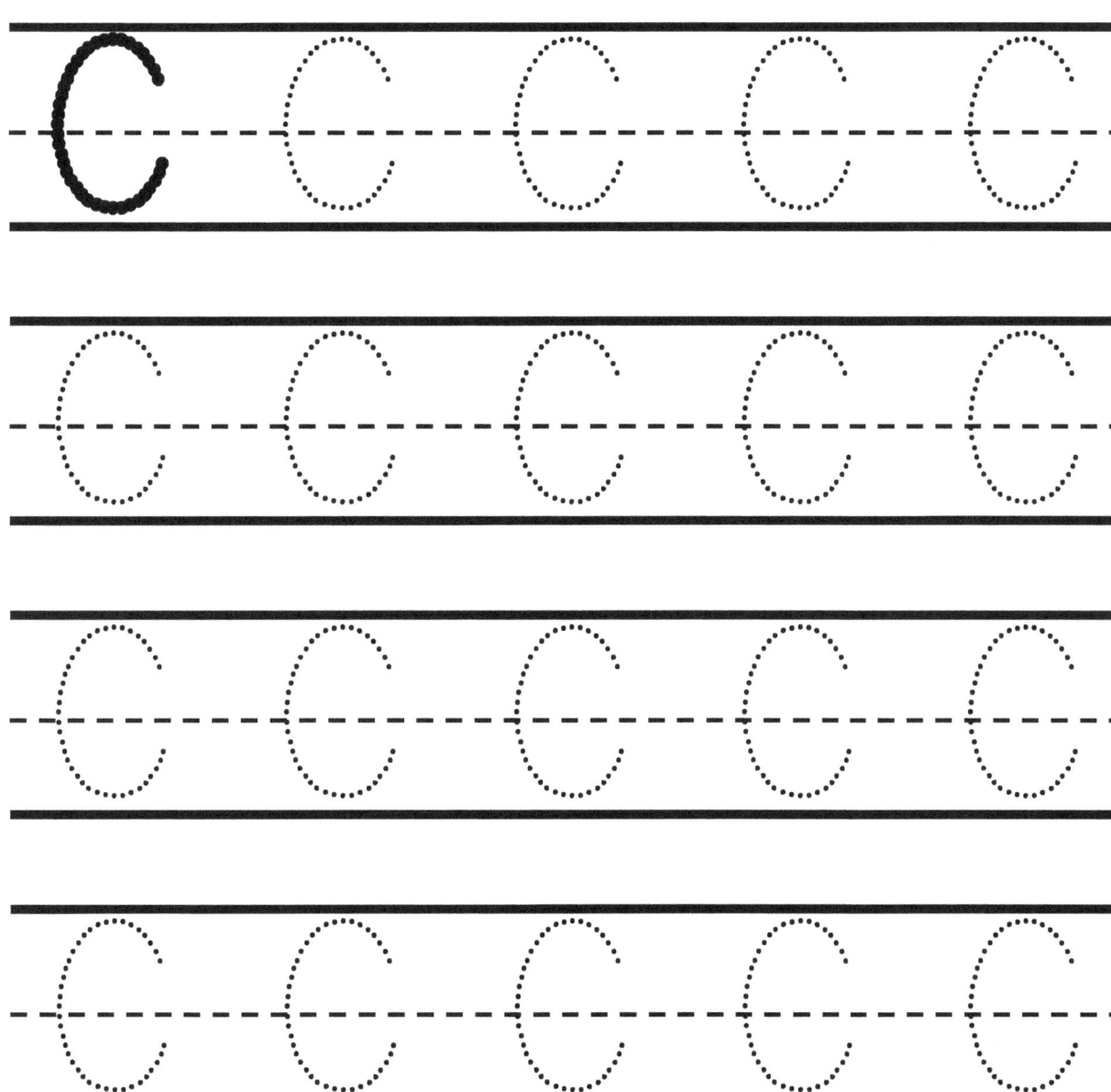

Duck

D D D D D D

D D D D D

D D D D D

D D D D D

Eat

Flag

Grouch

House

H

Icicle

Jump

J J J J J

J J J J J

J J J J J

J J J J J

Kick

K K K K K

K K K K K

K K K K K

K K K K K

Leg

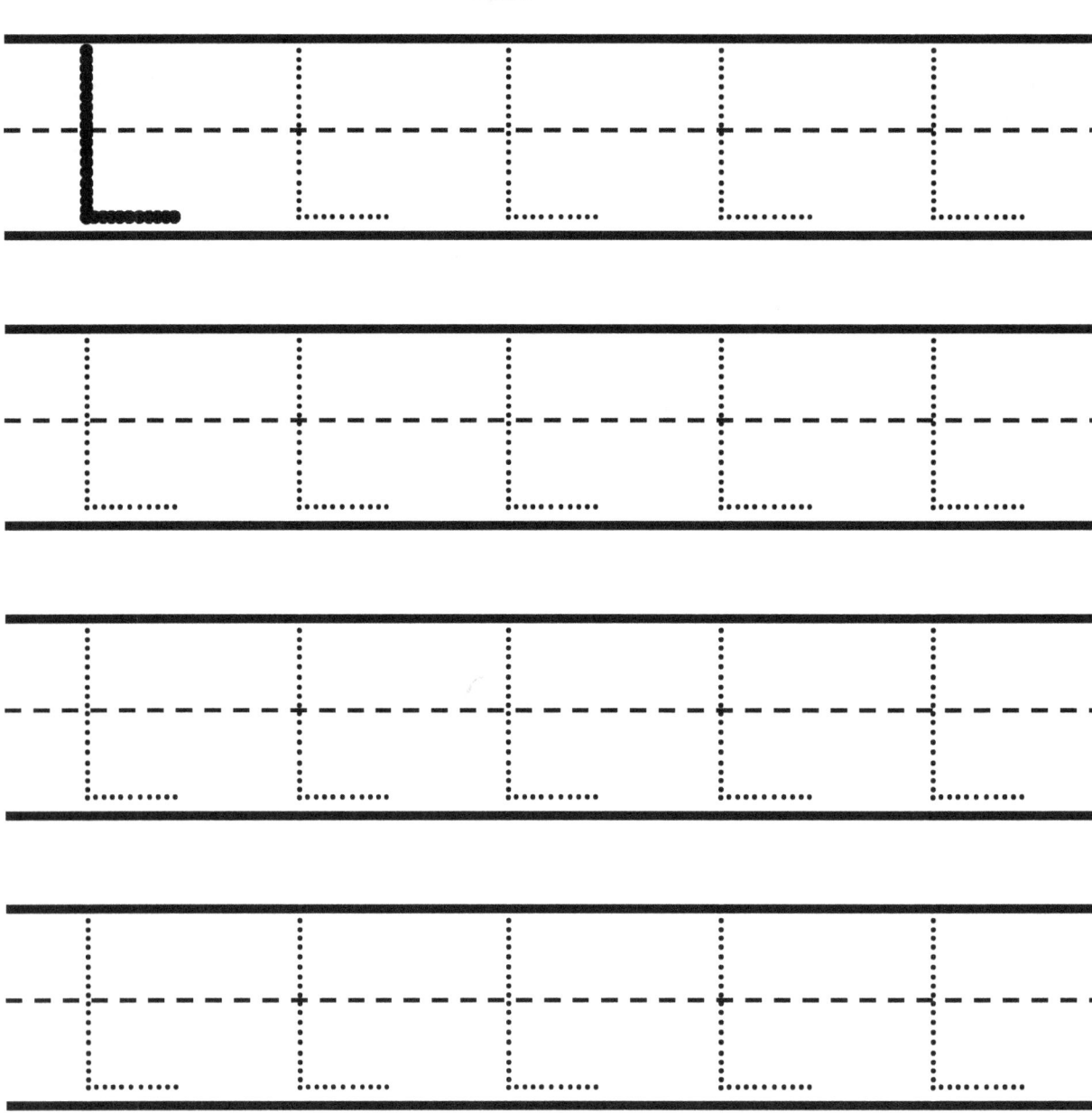

Mountains

Nose

Orange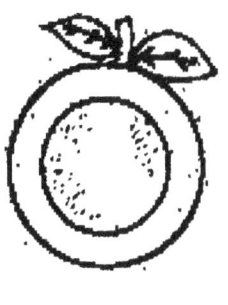

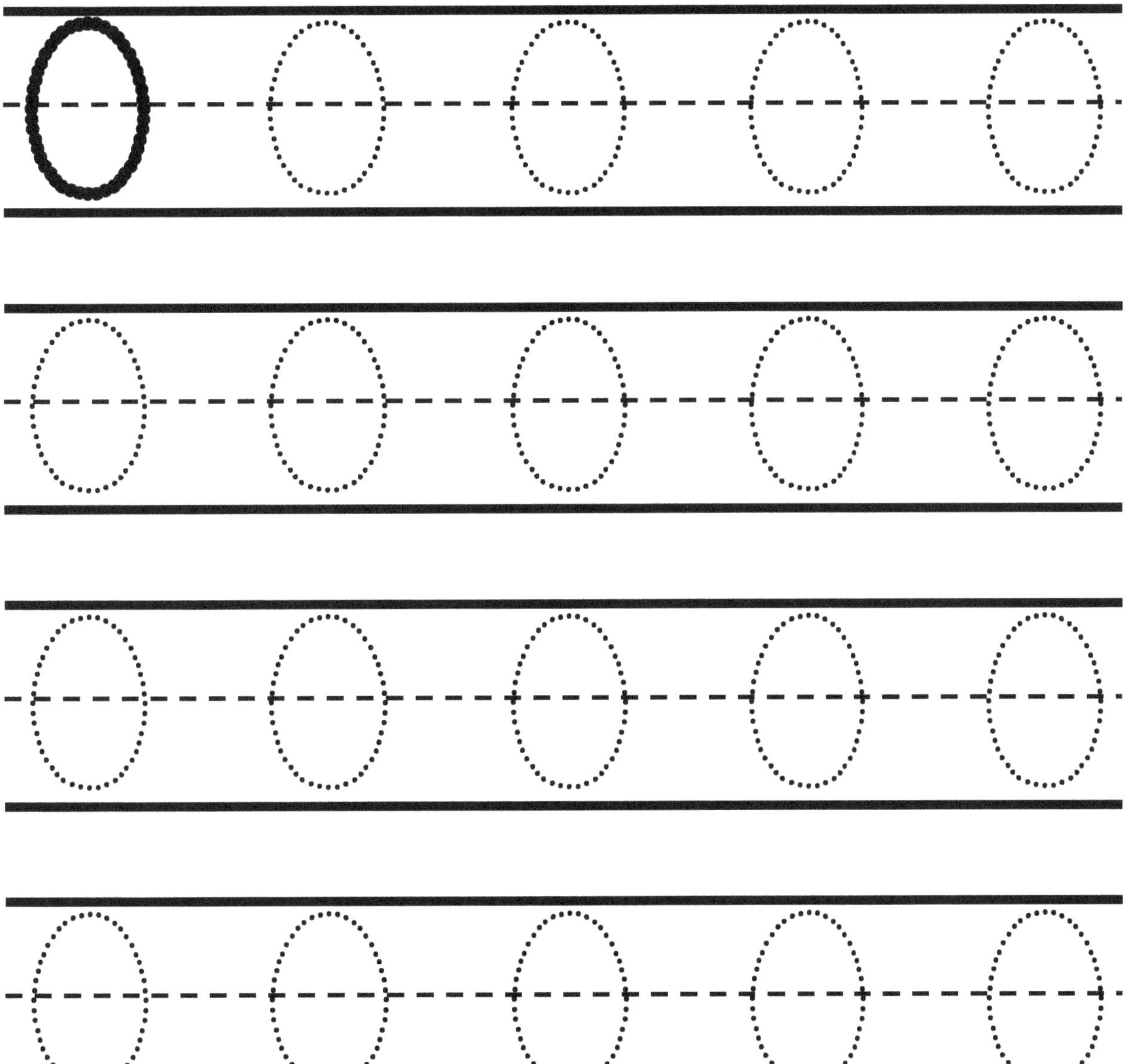

Pan

P P P P P

P P P P P

P P P P P

P P P P P

Queen

Q Q Q Q Q

Q Q Q Q Q

Q Q Q Q Q

Q Q Q Q Q

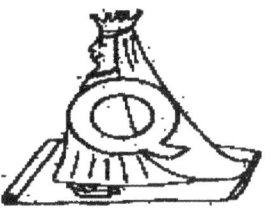

Run

R R R R R

R R R R R

R R R R R

R R R R R

Snake

S s s s s

s s s s s

s s s s s

s s s s s

Table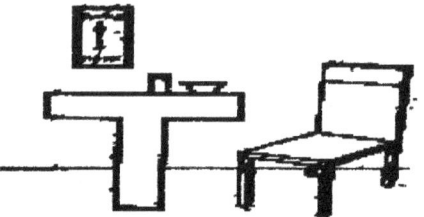

Ukulele

Vest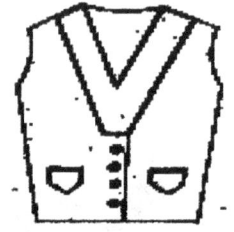

Wings

Xylophone

Yak

Y Y Y Y Y

Y Y Y Y Y

Y Y Y Y Y

Y Y Y Y Y

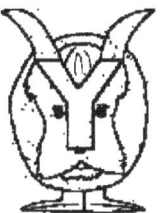

ZigZag

Alphabet

Aa Bb Cc Dd
Ee Ff Gg Hh
Ii Jj Kk Ll
Mm Nn Oo Pp
Qq Rr Ss Tt
Uu Vv Ww Xx
Yy Zz

www.ingramcontent.com/pod-product-compliance
Lightning Source LLC
Chambersburg PA
CBHW081324040426
42453CB00013B/2300